ATHLETE

MR. TOMONOSHi!

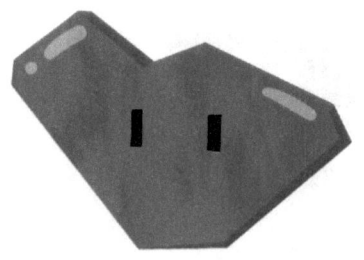

Copyright

© 2025 by TOMONOSHi LLC

All rights reserved. No part of this book may be reproduced, distributed, or transmitted in any form or by any means, including photocopying, recording, or other electronic or mechanical methods, without the prior written permission of the publisher, except in the case of brief quotations embodied in critical reviews and certain other noncommercial uses permitted by copyright law.

Title: *ATHLETE*

Written by: MR. TOMONOSHi!

Published by: TOMONOSHi LLC

ISBN 978-1-948760-07-2

For permissions and inquiries, contact:
mrtomonoshi@tomonoshi.com

REFLECTIONS

5. DEDICATION.

6. FOREWORD.

11. PROLOGUE: THE CALL OF THE JUNGLE.

15. THE ANIMAL WITHIN.

31. BECOMING THE ANIMAL.

38. THE FEMALE ATHLETE.

44. THE BLACK ATHLETE.

55. THE REFLECTION.

60. THE AUCTION.

66. GETTING THE MOST OUT OF YOUR ATHLETE.

74. THE SHORT LEASH.

78. THE MIND OF THE ANIMAL.

82. THE PREDATOR'S DILEMMA.

88. WHEN THE BODY BREAKS.

92. THE EXIT.

95. NATURE OF THE BEAST.

99. THE ANIMAL AT HOME.

105. REWIRING YOUR ATHLETE.

109. NEW BEAST.

115. THE PACK AND THE SILENCE.

118. AFTER THE PACK.

125. THE MATE.

129. EAT WHAT YOU KILL.

135. JUNGLE TO JUNGLE.

138. THE MANMADE JUNGLE.

143. ADAPT OR DIE.

148. EPILOGUE.

DEDICATION

To the animals I once ran
wild with.

FOREWORD

BY MARTELLUS BENNETT (MR. TOMONOSHi!)

Pro Bowl Tight End & Super Bowl Champion.

For as far back as I can remember, I've been an animal.

My animal of choice?
The Black Unicorn.

Powerful.

Majestic.

Magical.

  That's who I became my first year as a starter for the New York Giants, after leaving the Dallas Cowboys.

In Dallas, it felt like you could only be a horse.

Nothing else.

But in New York—under the leadership of the Giants—I felt something different.
I felt free.

Like a horse could become a unicorn. A horse with a colorful horn on its head.

That slight shift in atmosphere made all the difference. It was the first time I ever felt free as an athlete.

Maybe the last.

As an athlete, I experienced it all. I was the best animal at my position. I was the bottom animal at my position.

I was drafted.
Picked up.
Pro Bowl.
Suspended.
Traded.
Super Bowl.
Picked up again.
Cut.
Injured.
Sued.
Picked up again.
Injured again.
Retired.

I understand the athlete from a primal point of view. I've watched the animal from inside the jungle. And now—almost a decade removed from the jungle—I've had time to study it.

To analyze the animal. And the jungle that shaped it.

People often ask me: *What's it like to make it in the NFL? To be one of the best athletes in the world?*

This book is my answer.

Told in short, sharp chapters. Not just about the game—but about the animal. The system. The survival. The cost.

Because to understand the athlete, you have to understand the jungle. And to survive the jungle— you have to become something more than human.

You have to become an animal.

PROLOGUE: THE CALL OF THE JUNGLE

A FIELD GUIDE TO THE ATHLETE'S SOUL.

Every athlete carries a different energy.

A different rhythm.

A different instinct.

And if you watch closely—
you'll see the animal beneath the jersey.

    This is not about position.

        It's about presence.

  It's about what drives them.
        How they move.
      How they dominate.

Because the athlete is not born knowing what they are. They must hunt to discover it.

They must train.
They must suffer.
They must *listen*.

And when the time is right—
the jungle will call.

And the animal

        will answer.

Not all animals move the same.

Not all instincts strike the same chord.

But none of them know who they are until they move.

Until they compete.

Until they hunt.

> Because it is only in the hunt that the animal reveals itself.

> And once it does—
> there is no turning back.

The athlete becomes the beast.

The beast finds its jungle. And the jungle becomes home.

This book is about that journey.

The transformation.
The sacrifice.
The instinct.
The extinction.
And the evolution.

Because to understand the athlete, you must understand the animal.

And to understand the animal, you must return to the wild.

And once you do—you must hunt to survive.

THE ANIMAL WITHIN.

INSTINCT, IDENTITY, AND THE COST OF GREATNESS.

The athlete
is not just a competitor.

                      The athlete
              is a revelation.

They are the ones who remind us—viscerally, undeniably—that we are animals.

That beneath the suits, the screens, the systems, we are still made of muscle, bone, breath, and instinct.

Every human being is born an athlete.

It's survival of the fittest.

Every corner of the world demands something physical from the people born there.

There are humans who can hold their breath for minutes underwater.

Humans who can run for hours across desert plains.

Humans who scale cliffs with nothing but hands, feet, and raw will.

Athleticism is not a luxury.

> It's a language.
> A way of being.
> A way of surviving.

But the athlete—the one who trains, who competes, who performs—is something more.

Every time they step into the arena, they prove how magnificent the human body is.

They stretch the limits of what we thought possible.

They are evolution in motion.

This is what makes the Olympics so captivating.

Every few years, animals from every corner of the earth gather—not to wage war, but to compete.

To test strength, speed, precision.

To see which nation, which tribe, which lineage is the fittest.

>It's not just sport.
>It's ceremony.
>A ritual of movement.
>A global mirror held up to the human race.

The Olympics remind us that we are still animals—still bound by gravity, still ruled by time, still chasing the edge of what's possible.

And we do it through games.

Games that measure who can leap the farthest, strike the fastest, endure the longest.

Games that echo the hunt,

    the chase,

    the climb,

    the fight.

Every athlete is compared to an animal.

Sometimes casually—"That guy's an animal out there." Other times, precisely:

He's a bull in the paint.

She's a cheetah on the track.

He's got the wingspan of an eagle.

She's built like a panther.

These aren't just compliments.

They're classifications.

    They help us place the athlete on the food chain—in the ecosystem of the sport.

Who's the predator?
Who's the prey?

Who dominates the air, the ground, the water?

Who's apex?

It's how we make sense of greatness. We don't say someone is "very good."

We say they're a beast.

A monster.

A freak of nature.

Because deep down, we know: Sport is the last place where the jungle still lives.

Some athletes don't wait to be named. They choose their animal. They become it.

Kobe Bryant called himself the Black Mamba.

Not just for the speed or the strike—but for the mentality. Cold. Precise. Lethal under pressure. He studied the snake. He *became* the snake.

It wasn't a nickname. It was a philosophy.

Others are named by the world.

Mike Tyson was a pit bull—short, explosive, terrifying.

Serena Williams? A lioness. Power, grace, dominance.

Usain Bolt? A cheetah in human form.

Sha'Carri Richardson? A panther in full stride.

LeBron James? A mix of bull and eagle—force and flight.

These comparisons aren't random.

They're archetypes.
They help us understand what we're seeing. They help us *feel* it.

Because when an athlete is in their zone—locked in, untouchable, unstoppable—they don't look human.

They look wild.

We name our teams after beasts—
lions, tigers, hawks, bears—
not just for intimidation, but
because we know, deep down,
that sport is the last arena
where we allow ourselves to be
animals.

Where instinct is celebrated.

Where aggression is ritual.

The jungle isn't gone.
It's very much still here.
It's the arena.
It's the court.
The ring.
The field.
And the animal?

The animal is wearing a jersey.

But not everyone is ready for that truth.

> Especially when it comes to women.

One reason women's sports still struggle for recognition is because society isn't ready to see women as animals.

To do so would collapse the fragile ecosystem we've built—one that separates humans from the rest of the jungle, and women from the raw power of nature.

If both men and women are seen as animals, what happens to the illusion of control?

Of civility?

Of hierarchy?

In the WNBA, the animal energy is just as present—though rarely named aloud.

Brittney Griner? A great white—dominant in the paint, commanding space.

Diana Taurasi? A cobra—veteran venom, striking when it matters most.

Sabrina Ionescu? A hawk—visionary, sharp, always scanning the floor.

A'ja Wilson? An orca—majestic, calculating, and in total control of the waters she moves through. She doesn't overpower with noise—she overwhelms with presence. Smooth. Deadly. Unshakable.

But here's the thing: When men are called animals, it's praise.

When women are called animals, it's often discomfort.

Because to call a woman an animal is to admit she's powerful. And power in a woman still unsettles the system.

It doesn't matter—man or woman. To be an athlete is to tap into the animal within. To train your body to obey instinct.

To silence doubt.
To sacrifice comfort for dominance.

But to play long enough is to become inhuman in the eyes of others.

    The higher you climb, the
       more humanity you lose—
until you are no longer seen
             as a person,
           but a number,
              a jersey,

        a spectacle.

> They don't see your pain.
> They don't see your fear.
>> They can't fathom your sacrifice.
>>> They see stats.
>> They see highlights.

They see the animal they came to watch.

And when you stop performing—when the enthusiasm fades—they don't know what to do with you.

Because they never really knew you at all.

And the cruelest part? You can never quite fit back into society. Because society isn't built for animals like you.

You were apex—among prey. But now, the prey isn't yours to hunt.

You can't devour.
You can't chase.
You can't be what you were.

You are the wild animal in
the zoo.

> They'll paint the walls.
> They'll bring in trees and
> grass. They'll try to make it
> feel like home.

> But it's not.

You don't get to hunt.
You get fed—by human hands.
Measured portions.
Scheduled times.
For the rest of your
existence.

A tiger in Texas.
A lion behind glass in
Louisiana.
A cheetah on concrete in
Compton.

No wild animal is prepared
for the zoo.

Neither is the athlete.

Unlike wild animals, the human has imagination.

And the athlete? The athlete spends theirs early.

To make it professionally, you must begin imagining yourself in the championship long before you ever arrive.

> You see the lights.
> You hear the crowd.
> You feel the weight of the trophy in your hands—before your hands are even grown.

You give your imagination to that vision.

Day after day.

Year after year.

> Twenty-plus years of imagining.
>
> > Of becoming.

And for most, it never comes to fruition. They're exported to the zoo before they're ready to stop being wild. Before they've finished running. Before they've stopped believing.

So they bite.
They scratch.
They claw at the cage.
At the zookeepers.
At the zoo.
At the world.

>Because they don't know how to imagine themselves as anything else.

>>Animals.

This—this is the key.

To reclaim one's imagination. To dream again, not as a beast in pursuit of glory, but as a human in search of wholeness.

A small few make it.
They postpone their exportation.

They stay wild
a little longer.

But even they must one day
face domestication—the quiet
death of the wild.

The collar.

The cage.

The slow erasure of instinct.

They must one day be broken.

Not by injury.
Not by age.
Not by choice—by design.

           By civilization.

BECOMING THE ANIMAL.

WHAT THE GAME TAKES FROM THE HUMAN WHO PLAYS IT.

It takes everything to become an athlete at the highest level.

Not just time.

Not just talent.

It takes *you*.

Because when you decide to become the animal, you sacrifice the human version of yourself.

You begin the journey inward—
toward instinct,

toward dominance,

toward survival.

You become what the game demands.

And most athletes begin that journey young.

Too young to know who they really are.

Too young to have a foundation of self.

They don't know *who* they are—
they only know *what* they must
become.

Faster.
Stronger.
Smarter.
More durable.
More disciplined.
More animal.

To become, you must release
what you once were.

You shed your softness.
You silence your doubt.

You bury your humanity—just
to see how far you can go.

But if the system that molds
you only trains the animal—
if it ignores the human—then
you lose sight of your true
identity.

You become the animal full-
time.

And the ones who sacrifice
the most?

The ones who give everything to the transformation?

They become the wildest.

They become the kings and queens of the jungle.

But there's a cost.

Because while the body grows, and the instincts sharpen, the humanity lags behind.

You become great on the field or court—but underdeveloped in the game of life.

No tools for conflict.

No language for emotion.

No map for who you are when the lights go out.

You were trained to win.

Not to live.

You stepped out of the village and into the wild.

You left behind the rituals of ordinary life—the birthday parties, the sleepovers, the slow mornings—and entered the jungle of repetition, pressure, and performance.

You stopped playing for fun.

      You started hunting for purpose.

    You weren't raised like the others.

You were trained.

Conditioned.

Shaped into something
sharper,
faster,
more dangerous.

You became the animal.

And once you cross that line—once you've tasted the blood of competition, once you've felt the high of domination—you can't go back.

> You don't know how to sit still.

> You don't know how to be soft.

You don't know how to be *normal*.

Because you weren't raised in the village.

> You were raised in the jungle.

And the jungle doesn't raise humans.

> It raises animals.
> It doesn't teach manners.
> It teaches survival.
> It doesn't reward obedience.
> It rewards instinct.
> It doesn't ask you to fit in.
> It dares you to stay alive.

So when you walk into the village—with your eyes sharp, your body honed, your spirit unbroken—they don't know what to do with you.

> Because you weren't made for comfort.
>
> You were made for the hunt.
>
> And prey are afraid of the predator.
>
> That's the law of nature.

THE FEMALE ATHLETE.

WHY THE WORLD STILL FEARS HER.

When women become animals in
the eyes of society,
civilization begins to
tremble.

Because if *both* man and woman
are savage, then the whole
species is closer to the
jungle than we want to admit.

And we can't have that.

We've built too many systems
to pretend we've evolved
beyond the wild.

> So we prefer the feminine
> athlete to be graceful.
> Elegant.
> Controlled.

We celebrate the ballerina.
The figure skater.
The gymnast.

We call them swans.
Gazelles.
Butterflies.

Even when they dominate,
we reach for metaphors that
float—not ones that *hunt*.

Because to compare a woman to a predator would be to admit she has teeth.

That she stalks.
That she pounces.
That she *kills*.

And we're not ready for that.

Every major women's sports league will be met with resistance—not because the athletes aren't great, but because we are not ready to imagine women as the primal animals they are.

They are hunters.
They prowl.
They strike.
They roam the jungle,
stalking prey,
hunting for their next meal.

And until we see them as the animals they are, there will always be a discrepancy—in pay, in viewership, in respect.

Because deep down, the world isn't afraid women aren't strong enough.

It's afraid they're *just as savage* as men.

That they, too, can attack.
Compete.
Destroy.

And if that's true—if women are animals too—then the whole illusion collapses.

> The illusion that women are where we can always find humanity.
> Gentleness.
> Restraint.
> Control.

But nature tells a different story.

The mother bear is vicious.
The lioness leads the hunt.

The female orca is the apex predator of the sea.

In the wild, the female is
just as lethal—
just as strategic,
just as dominant
as her male counterpart.

And humans reject that truth.

Because the female athlete
doesn't just perform.

She reveals.

She shows us what the female
is capable of:
Speed.
Flight.
Power.
Tenacity.
The destruction of her prey.

    She is not the exception.
        She is the reminder.

Because when you empower the
animal in women, you force
the world to confront a
deeper truth:

That humanity itself is more
animal than we want to admit.

And that terrifies them.

THE BLACK ATHLETE.

BORN INTO THE JUNGLE. BUILT FOR THE HUNT.

If you happen to come across a Black athlete, you must understand what you're witnessing.

You're not just seeing talent.

You're seeing survival.

You're seeing someone whose reality has always been closer to the jungle.

The Black athlete is more primed for the training.

More wild.
More primal.
More willing to become the animal necessary to survive the jungle they were born into.

Because for them, the way of the animal—the hunt—has been fruitful.

It levels the playing field.
It removes the hierarchy of civilization.

>It rewards the best.
>The fastest.
>The strongest.
>The most relentless.

The laws of nature are fair.
Brutal, but fair.
And in a world where every other system resists them, this jungle makes sense.

This jungle is better suited for the Black athlete—because they face resistance in every other jungle.

>The corporate jungle.
>The academic jungle.
>The political jungle.
>The social jungle.

From a young age, the Black athlete is trained not just to live in the jungle—but to survive it.
To thrive in it.
To dominate it.

Because in the jungle, there
are no gatekeepers.

>Only predators.
>Only prey.

>And the Black athlete?
>They were born to hunt.

THE BLACK ATHLETE

THE STRUCTURED JUNGLE & THE RULES OF THE HUNT.

The Black athlete doesn't just
compete in the jungle. He
competes in a jungle organized
by animals unlike him.

A jungle where the terrain is
wild—but the rules are
manmade.

Because even here,
in the one place where
instinct should rule, the
white animal still dictates
the hunt.

Still decides who gets fed.
Who gets seen.
Who gets paid.

   The Black athlete may be the
   most dominant in the arena—
      but the arena is owned.

                  Governed.

                    Curated.

The white animal doesn't
always run the fastest.
Doesn't always jump the
highest.

> But they built the
> scoreboard.

They control the whistle.
They write the contracts.
They shape the narrative.

And so the Black athlete must
do more than perform.
They must decode.
Navigate.

Survive a jungle that was built
to exploit their bodies—and
profit from their performance.

They must be twice the beast
and twice the strategist. They
must hunt with precision
and speak with caution.
Because one wrong move, and the
system will remind them: this
is not your jungle.

> You're just allowed to run
> through it.

And because the Black athlete is seen as closer to the animal—closer to the savage—they are handled more inhumanely.

Their pain is minimized.
Their rage is criminalized.
Their body is commodified.
Their humanity is optional.

They celebrate their strength, but ignore their suffering. They love their speed, but question their intellect. They want the performance, but not the person.

Because when you see someone as an animal, you don't feel guilty when they're caged.

You don't flinch when they're broken.

You don't mourn when they're gone.

You just move on to the next one.

But here's the truth no one wants to say: The Black athlete shows just how powerful,
how majestic,
how courageous
the Black race truly is.

And that image must be curated.

Tamed.

Contained.

Because if the animal learns to think for itself—if the Black athlete begins to question the jungle—it will empower others in the zoo to do the same.

And that is dangerous to the manmade jungle.

That is a threat to the illusion of control.

So the Black athlete is taught to stay in line.

To be grateful.
To be obedient.
To hunt, but not to ask why.

To dominate, but not to dream
beyond the cage.

Because if they believe there
is no other jungle—no other
world where they can survive—
they will never leave.

They will become more animal.

                    Less human.

  Not because they are, but
because they were trained to
believe it's the only way to
              stay alive.

But what they forget—what
they always forget—is that
the Black athlete was born in
a different jungle.

One with sharper edges.

One that taught him how to
move in silence, how to
strike with purpose, how to
survive when the odds are
stacked.

The Black athlete doesn't
just win.
They disrupt.
They dominate.
They redefine what's
possible.
And that threatens the white
animals need to be king of
all animals.

And no matter how many rules
they write, no matter how
many cages they build—they
cannot out-hunt what was born
wild.

The black athlete will take
control of the jungle.

THE REFLECTION

WHO GETS TO BE KING OF THE JUNGLE.

Animals are drawn to animals who look like them.

The dog doesn't care what breed you are—it just knows you're dog.

There's recognition.

Kinship.

Instinct.

But history has shown us something else: The white animal prefers other white animals.

Not just out of comfort—but out of reflection.

They see themselves.

And so they deem them equal.

Familiar.

Worthy.

The white athlete is seen as closer to the owners of the jungle.

Closer to the architects.

Closer to the ones who built the scoreboard, who hold the keys to the cage.

They see more humanity in the white animal—because it mirrors their own.

And consciously or subconsciously, they want that animal to be king.

Just listen to the language.
The way they speak about the
white athlete:

"Smart."
"Disciplined."
"A student of the game."
"Leader."

Now listen to how they speak
about the Black athlete:

"Explosive."
"Raw talent."
"Athleticism."
"Natural ability."

One is praised for mind.
The other for muscle.

One is framed as evolved.
The other as instinctual.

Now look at who tells the
stories. Who writes the
headlines. Who sits in the
broadcast booth. Who shapes
the narrative of the jungle.

Who do they look most like?

Because the jungle may be wild—
but the story of the jungle is
curated.

And the crown is rarely handed
to the one who earned it.

It's given to the one who looks
like the king.

THE AUCTION.

THE MARKETPLACE WHERE ATHLETES BECOME ASSETS.

Once the animal is trained,
it must be sold.

The draft.
The combine.
The pro day.
The showcase.

It's not a celebration.
It's a marketplace.
An auction.

The athlete becomes stock.
Evaluated.
Measured.
Ranked.

>   They measure the feet.
>   The hands.
>   The wingspan.
>   The weight.
>   The gait.
>   The vertical.
>   The 40-yard dash.

They study the eyes.
The posture.
The twitch.
The temperament.

They ask: How much work can
we get out of this animal?

How long will it last?
How durable is the meat?
How obedient is the mind?

It's not personal.
It's business.
It's the ecosystem.

The athlete is no longer just
a body in motion—they are a
product in rotation.
A number on a board.
A projection on a screen.
A future asset.

And the ones who test well?

The ones with the perfect
frame, the rare speed, the
right pedigree?
They go early.
They go high.
They go expensive.

Because in this jungle, value
is everything.

And value is determined by
how much you can produce—not
how much you've endured.

But there's one thing they don't test for.

One thing they don't want to see.

How much humanity is left.

Because too much humanity? That's a red flag.

> If you cry too easily,
> if you think too deeply,
> if you speak too freely—
> you become a risk.

They don't want circus animals.

They want apex predators.

> They want the killer instinct.
> The cold stare.
> The silence before the strike.

They want the animal to be the animal—at all times.

No hesitation.
No softness.
No questions.

Because in this system,
empathy is a glitch.

Conscience is a complication.

And vulnerability?
That's a weakness they can't afford.

So the athlete learns to hide it. To tuck the humanity deep beneath the muscle.

> To perform the predator.
> To become the product.
>
> Because that's what gets drafted.
>
> That's what gets paid.
> That's what survives.

GETTING THE MOST OUT OF YOUR ATHLETE.

HOW TO BUILD THE ANIMAL YOU NEED.

Once you acquire an athlete,
you must begin developing its
mind.

Start young.

It can take years—sometimes
generations—to shape the
athlete into the animal you
need it to be.

> You must teach the athlete
> that it is a *privilege* to be
> an athlete.

> So that when it grows up,
> it believes it is a *privilege*
> to be punished.

To be pushed beyond limits.

To be broken—
mentally,
physically,
emotionally,
spiritually.

This will make the athlete
thirst to be broken.

Because the more it is broken, the more it will submit to the system.

The jungle you've designed for it. The one best suited for your needs.

The body must be fortified.

It must be built to withstand the beating it takes to perform.

A broken body makes you no money. An animal with a weak body is not worth the investment—unless you can buy low and flip it for a high return during its peak years.

Just get rid of the animal after it performs. You'll get more value in a trade.

Emotionally, you must teach
the animal not to cry. Not to
feel. The faster you
eliminate these, the faster
you can teach it to suppress
every emotion that doesn't
serve performance.

Build anger.
Build ego.

Teach it to celebrate the
ways of the jungle.

If you can get the athlete to
celebrate the very jungle
that breaks it, you can make
it feel anything you want—
whenever you want.

Spiritually,
the animal must worship the
jungle.
If they praise the very place
that breaks them,
they will be happy to
sacrifice
their mind,
their body,
their spirit,
their soul.

Reward your best athletes.
The most vicious.
The fastest.
The strongest.
The smartest.
The most skilled.

Shower them with everything
of value:
Praise.
Money.
Fame.

Put them on billboards.
In commercials.
In magazines.
In fashion shows.
On TV shows.
In movies.

Make them kings and queens of
your jungle.
Elevate them.
Celebrate them.
Promote them—not just to
honor them, but to bring more
people in to watch them
perform.

And more importantly—to make younger athletes *want* what they have.

To make them *sacrifice more* to get what you've given the best.

Every generation of athletes will perform better than the last.
They will be faster.
Stronger.
Harder.
More skilled.
More obedient.

Because the more you entice, the more they will have to become
to escape their own jungles.
To earn the crown.
To be seen.
To matter.

This will increase the longevity of your business.
It will keep the pipeline full.

Don't worry about the upfront
cost—in a hundred years,
it'll be pennies out of your
pocket.

But be careful—do not
overfeed your animal.

If you give it too much, it
will begin to believe it has
power.

And that belief is dangerous.

It is detrimental to your
business.

If this occurs,
immediately divest in a few
of your investments.
Pull the endorsements.
Cancel the contracts.
Take it all away.

This will save you more money
than it will cost you.
It will remind the others.
It will restore the order.

And above all—never let an animal own a jungle that can feed the other animals as well as you can.

Never let them build something that makes the others question your necessity.

Because if one animal learns to feed the pack, it will reshape the minds of all animals in all jungles.

It will destroy years of investment.

It will collapse the illusion.

Let them taste it—but never let them own it.

If you can train your animal in these ways—you will get the most out of your athlete.

THE SHORT LEASH.

*HOW TO CONTROL THE ANIMAL
WITHOUT LOSING A HAND.*

The short leash is the worst
thing for the animal.

Fear the short leash.

It keeps the animal too close
to the hand—too close to the
teeth.

      The lack of space the
constant tension the pressure
on the neck—it will lead the
            animal to bite.

    It is better to let the
animal believe it is leading.
Better to let it believe it
           is free.

      You lengthen the leash.
      You widen the fence.

You give it space—not because
  it deserves it, but because
    it won't search for more.

If the animal believes it has
its own jungle,
it won't try to escape.
It won't test the boundaries.
It won't bite the hand.

You maintain control without the struggle the short leash demands.

And most importantly—you keep both hands.

But if the animal decides to leave the boundaries you've created, do not chase it.

Let it go.

It will likely return.
It will realize it cannot survive outside the jungle you built for it to be king.

And if it doesn't return—if it finds a way to become king or queen of another jungle—you never wanted that animal anyway.

Because that animal is dangerous. That animal will destroy the hierarchy you created. That animal will expose the illusion.

And there are plenty more
            athletes.

            Maybe cheaper.
            Maybe quieter.
      Maybe easier to leash.

THE MIND OF THE ANIMAL.

WHEN THE WILD MIND NO LONGER FITS THE WORLD.

The athlete doesn't think like other humans.

Because apex predators don't think like herbivores.

> The hunger is different.
> The focus is sharper.
> The hunt is more primal.

Over time, the athlete develops a mind built on routine.

From childhood to adulthood, life operates inside a system:

Train.

Eat.

Recover.

Compete.

Repeat.

The mind becomes a machine—wired for discipline, calibrated for performance, conditioned to win.

Athletes are trained to find
weaknesses—in their
opponents,
in themselves,
in the environment—and
exploit them.

They are surrounded by others who think the same way.

The locker room becomes a sanctuary.

A jungle within the jungle.

A place where the language of dominance is understood.

But when the athlete is removed from that space—
when the season ends,
when the career ends,
when the uniform is gone—
they suffer.

Mentally.
Emotionally.
Existentially.

Because the world outside the locker room doesn't speak their language.

It doesn't move at their pace.

It doesn't understand their hunger.

A dolphin in the zoo knows it's not in the ocean.

>It knows the difference.
>
>So does the athlete.
>
>They may smile.
>They may adapt.
>But deep down, they know:
>
>This isn't the wild.
>This isn't home.

THE PREDATOR'S DILEMMA.

INSTINCT, EMPATHY, AND THE SHAME OF OPPORTUNITY.

Emotionally, it gets…
strange.
Twisted.
Honest.

You're the backup.
You've been waiting.

Training.
Starving for a chance to hunt.

And then it happens—the starter goes down.

Injury.

Pain.

A moment of silence.

And inside you?
A flicker of joy.
A surge of adrenaline.
A quiet, shameful *yes*.

You care.
You really do.
But you're also glad.
Because now—it's your turn.

This is the emotional rift
the athlete must live with.

The duality of instinct and empathy.

The animal and the human.

Those who choose the human—who hesitate, who feel too much—they don't last long.

The game doesn't reward softness.

But those who move forward with the thought: *If I play well enough, they'll never get their spot back...*

Those are the ones who rise. And with every step forward, they lose a little more of their humanity.

Because the game doesn't just ask for your body.

It asks for your soul.

And sometimes, it asks you to root for someone else's downfall—just so you can rise.

That's not evil.
That's the ecosystem.
That's the jungle.

Animals hunt.
Animals move on.
They don't wait for the weak.
They don't nurse the injured.
They don't bury their dead.

Only humans do that.

Only humans pause to grieve.

To tend.
To remember.

But the athlete?
The athlete lives somewhere
in between.

Because in the world of
sport, mourning is a luxury.

Compassion is a risk.

And stillness is a threat.

Animals mourn in motion.
And so do athletes.

There are no mental health
days in the jungle.

No timeouts for grief.
No space for softness.

And when an athlete *does*
pause—when they speak up, sit
out, ask for help—they are
seen as the weak link in the
herd.

>A liability.
>A break in the chain.

The message is clear:
Keep moving.
Keep hunting.

>Or be left behind.

And you *will* be left behind.
By your teammates.
By your coaches.
By your organization.
By the fans.
By the city.
By the jungle.

There is no room for stillness.

No reward for reflection.

No mercy for the wounded.

There is no sanctuary in the wild.

No safe space for the broken.
No pause button for pain.

  There is only the next game.
               The next rep.

     The next body to outpace,
            outlast, outdo.

And if you can't keep up—
you're not just benched.

You're discarded.

You're excommunicated from the pack—left to die in the tall grass.

Because in the jungle, memory is short.

And mercy is extinct.

WHEN THE BODY BREAKS.

THE COLLAPSE OF THE TEMPLE THAT MADE YOU GOD.

The athlete's value has been
tied to the performance of
the body.
Not the mind.
Not the heart.
Not the soul.
The body.

How fast you run.
How high you jump.
How far you throw.
How accurate you kick.

That's what made you matter.
That's what got you paid.
That's what made people
cheer.

But when the body can no
longer perform—
when the knees ache,
when the speed fades,
when the injuries pile up—the
value disappears.

And with it, the self-worth.

> Because in the jungle,
> when the animal can no longer
> hunt, it loses its place in
> the pack.

Same with the athlete.

You're no longer useful.
No longer feared.
No longer needed.

And the worst part?

> None of the physical gifts
> that made you great mean
> anything in the world
> outside.

There's no bonus in the office for a 40-inch vertical.

No promotion for a 4.3 forty.

No corner office for a perfect spiral.

The body that once made you a god is now just a memory.

A relic.

A résumé no one reads.

And if you were never taught to value anything beyond the body—if you were never taught to build a self beyond the sport—then what's left?

Just a broken, worthless animal, whose greatest hunts are deemed to be behind it.

An animal no longer feared, no longer worshipped, no longer of value.

An animal that will drown in the riverbank of memory, as they try—desperately—to learn how to hunt again.

THE EXIT.

FROM SURVIVAL TO LEGACY.

The animal must prepare to leave the jungle *before it is forced out.*

Because no matter how sharp the claws, how fast the sprint, how loud the roar—the jungle always moves on.

There will always be a younger predator.
A fresher body.
A louder name.

And if you wait too long,
if you cling too tightly,
you won't leave the jungle with honor—you'll be dragged out in silence.

  So the wise animal begins the
                 exit early.
              Not in fear.
          But in foresight.

They begin to build a life beyond the hunt.

They begin to plant roots outside the roar.

They begin to imagine a self
that isn't measured by stats,
or speed,
or spotlight.

Because leaving the jungle
isn't weakness.

It's evolution.

It's the moment the animal
becomes the elder.

> The teacher.
> The builder.
> The guide.

It's the moment the roar
becomes a voice.

The instinct becomes wisdom.
The survival becomes legacy.

And when the animal leaves on
its own terms—with grace,
with clarity, with purpose—it
doesn't lose its power.

It *reclaims* it.

NATURE OF THE BEAST.

*WHEN HUMAN NATURE COLLIDES
WITH THE ATHLETE'S CODE.*

The athlete's nature is not like everyone else's.

It's not built on comfort.
It's not built on compromise.
It's built on performance.

Stats don't lie.
That's the wild.
That's the code.

You train.
You execute.
You win—or you don't.
And everything you get is earned.

> But the world outside the arena?

It's not built for wildlife.

It's built for politics.
For relationships.
For knowing the right people,
not being the right person.

In the jungle, the strongest leads.

In the office, the most liked does.

The athlete walks into this world—surrounded by humans who say they want greatness, but have long since settled for stability.

They say they want to grow, but they don't want to sweat.

They say they want to lead, but they don't want to hunt.

And the athlete?

They don't know how to settle.

They don't know how to coast.
They don't know how to play the game of appearances.

Because their entire life has been performance-based.
Not politics.
Not perception.
Just production.

But in this new world, performance isn't always rewarded.

Excellence isn't always recognized.

And truth?
Truth is often inconvenient.

So the athlete struggles.

Not because they're unqualified—but because they're *overqualified* in the wrong currency.

They speak the language of results. But the world speaks the language of relationships.

And in that mismatch, the beast begins to feel caged again.

Because the wild doesn't reward charm.

It rewards *execution*.

THE ANIMAL AT HOME.

HOW DO YOU CAGE WHAT WAS BORN TO ROAM?

> When the animal returns home
> from the wild, it's not just
> an adjustment for the
> athlete—it's an adjustment
> for the entire family.

Because this isn't the same person who left.

This is someone who's lived by instinct.
By routine.
By adrenaline.
By war.

And now?

There's no outlet.
No arena.
No hunt.

The body still twitches with energy.

The mind still scans for threats.

The heart still beats like it's game day.

But there's nowhere to run.

Nowhere to strike.
Nowhere to stretch.

The wild animal is in the house.

And the family—they've never met this version before.

They knew the competitor.
They knew the champion.
But they've never lived with the caged version.
The restless version.
The version that doesn't know what to do with stillness.

Nor has the athlete.

No animal wants to be caged. And the caging of every wild animal is the same—frantic, chaotic, confused.

The animal doesn't understand the walls. It doesn't understand the silence. It doesn't understand why the hunt has stopped.

It paces.
It lashes out.
It shuts down.

And the athlete is no different.

They've spent their life in motion—measured by output, defined by performance.

Now they're still.

Now they're home.

But they don't know how to *be* home.

Because the jungle taught them how to survive—but not how to rest.

Not how to connect.

Not how to live without the roar.

There's no playbook for this.

No training camp for reintegration.

No warning for what it feels like when the jungle follows you home.

Because how does a lion adjust to the zoo?

How does a dolphin adjust to a tank?

How does a wild animal adjust to domestic life?

It needs space.
It needs movement.
It needs purpose.

      But the house is small.
         The routine is gone.
  And the world no longer asks
           for the animal—
     it asks for the human.

The problem is, the human was never fully formed.

The human was buried beneath the training, beneath the discipline, beneath the chase.

Now the world wants
conversation instead of
competition.

Softness instead of strength.
Presence instead of
performance.

But the athlete only knows
how to hunt.

Only knows how to win.

Only knows how to *be* the
animal.

So they sit in the house,
in a body built for war,
in a world that no longer
wants to fight.

And they wonder:
What now?

REWIRING YOUR ATHLETE.

TRAINING THE IMPULSE WITHOUT KILLING THE INSTINCT.

Any animal in an unknown environment is more dangerous than it is in its own habitat.

It will be in survival mode. It will bite.

It will act with aggression—not out of malice, but out of confusion.

Out of fear.

Out of no longer having a master.

The bite becomes a way to feel in control. To establish dominance the only way it knows how: through violence.

Do not allow the athlete to get away with snapping back, yapping, or any other signs of aggression.

Because when the athlete bites, they are trying to become king of a jungle they do not yet understand.

And that confusion will cause them to act out.

But when the athlete bites—
they must learn *why* they've bitten.

Not just that they struck—
but what triggered the strike.

What wound was touched.
What fear was awakened.
What memory was pulled from the bone.

Because the animal doesn't always know.
It reacts.
It protects.
It survives.

But survival is not the same as mastery.

The athlete must evolve.
They must accept training—
not just of the body,
but of the impulse.

Because if the animal is
never trained, it becomes
dangerous. Not just to
others—but to itself.

The bite must be studied.
The root of the attack must
be understood.

Was it pride?
Was it fear?
Was it pain disguised as
power?

This is not about becoming
soft. It's about becoming
aware.

The animal must not be
silenced. But it must be
rewired.

Because true strength is not
just knowing how to strike—
but knowing *when not to*.

NEW BEAST.

*HOW THE ATHLETE EVOLVES
WITHOUT LOSING THE HUNT.*

The athlete must learn to
turn down their primal
instincts.

Not to erase them—
but to *refine* them.

This is the task of
domesticating a wolf.
It takes centuries.

But the athlete doesn't have
centuries.

                They have *moments*.

They must adjust immediately—
or fall behind just as fast.

Because for years, the
athlete has trained the body.

                        The heart.
                        The spirit.

They've mastered recovery,
nutrition, performance.

But they've fallen behind in
the skills required to thrive
in other arenas.

They haven't studied the politics of the boardroom. They haven't trained in the language of influence. They haven't learned how to hunt in a world where charm beats strength.

And the truth is—most of the world's leaders wouldn't last a day in the jungle.

They couldn't survive a single round,

a single hit,

a single sprint.

But fitness isn't a requirement to lead a Fortune 500 company.

It is to lead a billion-dollar sports organization. And that's where the disparity becomes *gargantuan*.

Because while the athlete's body has an expiration date, the CEO's game has no clock.

They've been hunting
relationships for decades.
They've been swimming in
these waters since birth.

A shark on land is no longer
a predator.

A lion in the water is no
longer the king of the
jungle.

But here's the good news:
Some wolves have learned to
swim.
Some beasts have evolved.
And the best hunters?
They always find a meal.

This is the way of nature.

The athlete must not suppress
their instincts.

They must *redirect* them.
They must become a new beast.
Learn new ways to hunt.

New ways to win.

Because the minute the
athlete loses their drive—
they begin to die.
Slowly. Quietly.
From the inside out.

The hunter must hunt.

The gym won't be enough.
The mirror won't be enough.
The applause won't be enough.

They need a new game.
A new arena.
A new mountain to climb.

Because only when the athlete
has a mountain to climb,
a prey to chase, a purpose to
pursue—will they feel whole
again.

The athlete must not become a
wolf in sheep's clothing.
They must become a wolf
proudly wearing sheep.

Not to deceive—
but to navigate.
To move through new terrain
without losing their nature.

Because pretending to be
something you're not?

That's weakness.

But adapting while staying
true to your instincts?

That's evolution.

Let the world see the wool.
Let them underestimate.
Let them assume you've
softened.

Because underneath?
The teeth are still sharp.
The hunger is still real.
The hunt is still alive.

You're not hiding.
You're *hunting differently*

THE PACK AND THE SILENCE.

ON LONELINESS, LOYALTY, AND THE SEARCH FOR KIN.

The animal will struggle to
find a new pack.

There aren't many animals
like him in the suburbs.
Not many who've run the
jungle.

Not many who've hunted.
Not many who *understand*.

    He tries to stay in touch—
         with the old pack.
 The ones who knew the hunger.
 The ones who knew the rhythm.
     The ones who knew *him*.

It brings a sense of
normalcy.
A flicker of the old fire.
A reminder that he wasn't
dreaming.

But the pack doesn't always
respond.
They're scattered now.
Tamed.
Busy.
Gone.

And so the animal feels it—the loneliness.

Because hunting alone was never the ideal way to hunt. It was always about the chase *together*.
The shared breath.
The shared blood.
The shared purpose.

Watching the old pack hunt from afar
can only do so much.
It stirs the memory,
but it doesn't feed the soul.

So the animal has a choice:

> Move forward—and learn to hunt in this new jungle. Or return—to the old one, where it all made sense.
>
> But either way, the animal must hunt. Because stillness is death. And the pack— whether old or new—is not just about company.
>
> It's about *survival*.

AFTER THE PACK.

ON LONELINESS, LOYALTY, AND
THE SEARCH FOR KIN.

The athlete has always been a
pack animal.
Trained to hunt with others
just like them.
One goal.
One mission.
One heartbeat.

    The pack was everything—
teammates, coaches, staff,
a tribe forged in sweat and
survival.

But when the animal migrates
into new territory, the pack
stays behind.

You may cross paths again.
You may exchange nods,
memories, old war stories.
But the truth is—the pack was
only a pack because of
proximity and purpose.

    Once those are gone,
so is the bond.

    And for the pack animal,
this is devastating.

Because now, you're alone.
No more huddles.
No more war cries with the pack.

No more shared hunger.

Just silence.

And finding a new pack?
That's not easy.

A goldendoodle could never understand a wolf.

> It hasn't tasted the wild.
> It hasn't felt the freedom.
> It's never known the joy of the first bite of the hunt.
> It's only known kibbles and bits.

So the athlete walks alone.
Misunderstood.
Mistranslated.
Mismatched.

But the truth is—no animal is meant to be alone forever.

Not even the apex predator.

It's *imperative* that the athlete finds a new pack.

Because the loneliness?
It can be lethal.

You've never not had a pack before. Never not had a shared mission. Never not had a reason to run.

And as the animal prepares to come home from the wild, the family must begin the work of integration.

Because the time spent in the jungle has stripped away the rhythms of domesticated life.

The animal will need space.
It will need patience.

But most of all—it will need to feel *useful*.

It will need to feel *part of something*.

Because usefulness is purpose.

And purpose is survival—not
in the jungle, but in the
quiet.

The animal doesn't need
applause.

It needs *meaning*.
It needs to know that its
instincts still matter,
that its strength still
serves, that its presence
still protects.

    Contribution to the home,
to the community, to society—
this is how the animal begins
    to reclaim its humanity.

Not by forgetting the wild,
but by *translating* it.

The discipline becomes mentorship.

The leadership becomes guidance.

The hunger becomes vision.

The instinct becomes intuition.

This is how the animal becomes whole again.

Not by being tamed—but by being *seen*.

Not as a relic of the jungle, but as a force for something greater.

Because even after the hunt is over, the animal still has something to give.

And when it finds a place to give it—it finds a reason to stay.

This is what the animal desires, even if it is unable to communicate its desires.

THE MATE.

LOVING THE ANIMAL AFTER THE HUNT.

The mating partner of the
animal must be equipped to
handle what the world has
spent years suppressing.

They have the hardest task.

Because after years of
breaking, the broken animal
will need to be healed.

Cared for.

Understood.

The attitude of the animal
will be unpredictable. Its
moods will shift like
weather. Its silence will
speak louder than its words.

Because the ability to
communicate emotion—that was
broken too.

The partner must learn to
read the animal's body
language.

The twitch of a muscle.
The drop of the shoulders.
The stillness in the eyes.
These are the new vocabulary.

A good partner will guide the
animal into a new world.

An unequipped mate will lose
the animal
to new jungles.

The partner must be strong—
not just physically, but
emotionally.

Spiritually.

They must be aware.

Present.
One step ahead.

They must know what the
athlete feels before the
athlete can articulate it.

But they must not rush the
animal to the answer. They
must not force the healing.

They must be a guide.

A mirror.
A safe place.

Using a reward system—a
"treat" system—can help
establish trust.

It creates structure
without control. It offers
direction without domination.

Because the animal must not
feel caged again.

>   It must feel chosen.
>   Seen.
>   Safe.

This is not about taming the
animal.

It's about helping it
remember that it is more than
what it was trained to be.

EAT WHAT YOU KILL.

THE COST OF FEEDING THE PACK.

There's one thing every animal must learn to navigate: *If I go out and eat—who deserves a piece?*

In the wild, the answer is simple.

The strongest eats first.
The hunter eats what they kill.

No animal stows food for the previous generation.

No lion saves meat for its elders.

Survival comes first.
The hunt must continue.

But the athlete?
The athlete is different.

Because while they've lived like an animal, they still crave something only humans can give: *connection.*

So they stay close to their family. To the people who remind them of who they were before the jungle.

Before the beast. Before the transformation.

They bring home the kill—the contract, the check, the championship—and they share it.

Not because it's required. But because it's *human*.

Because giving makes them feel grounded. Because saying yes keeps them tethered to the people who still see the child beneath the champion.

They're not just paying bills.

They're paying to feel human.

And so they say yes.

Yes to the cousin who needs
help.

Yes to the friend with the
business idea.
Yes to the parent who says
they sacrificed everything.

Because how do you say no
to the people who were there
before the spotlight?

  How do you deny the ones who
                remind you
        you were once human?

You say yes—not just out of
love, but out of fear.

Fear of losing them.
Fear of seeming ungrateful.
Fear of becoming the animal
full-time.

So you give.
And give.
And give.

Until the giving becomes
expected.

Until the yes becomes
currency.

Until the love feels like a transaction.

They say yes until it's too late.

Until the money runs dry.
Until the resentment sets in.
Until the animal is drained—not just financially, but emotionally.

Because no one taught them how to say no.

No one told them that even the strongest must eat first.

That in order to keep hunting, you have to protect the hunter.

And by the time you realize what's happened—you're not just broke.

You're hollow.

Because you weren't just paying bills.

You were paying to stay connected.

Paying to feel seen.
Paying to feel *human*.

JUNGLE TO JUNGLE.

THE JUNGLE'S LESSONS FOR A CIVILIZED WORLD.

Although the physical skills used to dominate the game hold little value in the civilized world—there is *plenty* of wisdom the athlete carries forward.

They just have to learn how to see it.

Because beneath the speed, beneath the strength, beneath the spectacle— there are tangibles.

Discipline.
Hard work.
Teamwork.
Strategy.
Leadership.
Adaptability.

The ability to study, to prepare, to execute under pressure.

These are not just athletic traits.

They are *life skills*.
They are *business skills*.
They are *human skills*.

The athlete has spent a
lifetime mastering them—they
just didn't know they were
doing it.

They thought they were
learning how to win games.
But they were learning how to
lead.

How to sacrifice.
How to show up when it's
hard.
How to build trust.
How to bounce back from
failure.

The jungle taught them more
than how to hunt.

It taught them how to *endure*.
How to *evolve*. How to listen.
How to move with purpose.

And now, in this next phase—
that wisdom is the bridge.
From instinct to insight.
From survival to
significance.

From the animal to the whole.

THE MANMADE JUNGLE.

WHY THE ANIMAL STRUGGLES TO ADAPT.

The athlete is intelligent.
It can learn.
And it can learn quickly.

Show the animal a task—and it
will master the task.
Not just through repetition,
but through instinct,
attention, and adaptation.

> But an environment without
> clarity—without honest,
> unapologetic direction or
> feedback—will hinder the
> animal's ability to learn.
> To execute.
> To evolve.

The jungle is honest.
The hunt is clear.
There is no confusion in
nature.

Only consequence.

> But the new jungle—the
> civilian jungle—doesn't
> operate with clarity.
>
> The rules are fickle.
> The goals are hidden.

The hunters hide their hands.
Their intentions.
Their prey.

Here, the hunt is led by manipulation.

By politics.
By performance without purpose.

This is not the way of the jungle.

Not the way of nature.
Not the way of the animal.

It is the way of the human.

And so the athlete—the animal—must now learn to navigate a manmade jungle.

One where instinct alone is not enough.

Where survival requires translation. Where clarity must be carved from confusion.

Because in this jungle, the strongest don't always win. The smartest don't always lead. And the honest don't always survive.

ADAPT OR DIE.

WHY THE ANIMAL MUST EVOLVE TO STAY ALIVE.

The animal must adapt to survive.

Because adaptability *is* sustainability.

> The climate will change.
> The terrain will shift.
> The nature around the animal will evolve.

So the animal's nature must evolve too.

This isn't weakness.
This is *wisdom*.

This is not a flaw.
This is the design.

The athlete is built for this.

They've adapted their entire life.

New roles. New rules. New rivals. Strategies shift.
Game plans diverge.
Those who adapt will survive.
Those who don't will die.

This is the way of nature.

The athlete will thrive—*if* they find a way to keep the animal alive.

Because if the animal within goes extinct, so will the athlete.

But it's bigger than that.

The animal in *us* must stay alive in order for us—as a species—to survive.

And the athlete? The athlete awakens the animal in us all.

This is why we watch.
Why we cheer.
Why we pay them so much.

Not just for entertainment.
But for remembrance.

To be reminded of the animals we were.

The animals we *are*.

That we are still at the top
of the food chain.
That the human body is still
capable of greatness.
Of power.
Of beauty.
Of dominance.

The athlete is not just a
competitor.

They are a mirror.
A memory.
A myth.

And when they pass that
instinct on—to their
offspring, to their
ancestors, to the next
generation of beasts—the
cycle continues.

>   And we're all so lucky.
>   Lucky to witness it.
>   Lucky to cheer for it.

Lucky to watch the next
generation of animals rise.

THE END.

EPILOGUE.

FOR THE ONES WHO NEVER LEFT THE JUNGLE.

This is for the animals who never made it out.

The ones who were broken before they could evolve.
The ones who were used, then discarded.

The ones who were told to be strong—but never taught how to heal.

This is for the ones who gave everything and were left with nothing.

For the ones who were trained to perform but never taught to feel.

For the ones who were crowned jungle kings but never shown how to be human again.

This is for the quiet ones.

The angry ones.

The ones who vanished.

The ones who still run—not
toward glory, but away from
pain.

This is for the athlete who
still hears the roar
even in the silence.
Who still feels the leash
even when it's gone.

You are not forgotten.
You are not alone.
You are not just what you
were trained to be.

You are still an animal.
Still alive.
Still evolving.

And if you ever find your way
out of the jungle—
we'll be waiting.
Not with applause.
But with understanding.
With space.
With fire.
With kin.

Because the story doesn't end
with the hunt.

It begins again
with the return.

with love + imagination

-MR. TOMONOSHi!

www.ingramcontent.com/pod-product-compliance
Lightning Source LLC
Chambersburg PA
CBHW022013160426
43197CB00007B/407